FRIDGE

RENARD PRESS — PLAYSCRIPT I

FRIDGE: ORIGINAL READING AT ETCETERA THEATRE IN 2016, WITH THERICA WILSON-READ, SIÂN BENNETT AND LEO GARRICK, DIRECTED BY TONJE WIK OLAUSSEN. ORIGINAL PRODUCTION AT KING'S HEAD THEATRE IN 2017, DIRECTED BY TONJE WIK OLAUSSEN WITH BLACKOUT CREATIVE ARTS AND MUSIC BY PHOEBE ROBINSON. LO PLAYED BY MARY O'LOAN, ALICE PLAYED BY EMMA ZADOW AND CHARLIE PLAYED BY LEO GARRICK.

SPECIAL THANKS TO RACHEL HOSKER, ARTHUR VELARDE, EDWARD WATCHMAN, GABRIELLE DE SAUMAREZ, IZZY DAWS AND ANOUSHKA BONWICK.

FRIDGE

EMMA ZADOW

RENARD PRESS

RENARD PRESS LTD

Kemp House
152–160 City Road
London EC1V 2NX
United Kingdom
info@renardpress.com
020 8050 2928

www.renardpress.com

Fridge first published by Renard Press Ltd in 2021

Text © Emma Zadow, 2021
Cover design by Will Dady

Paperback ISBN: 978-1-80447-007-7
e-book ISBN: 978-1-913724-46-7

Emma Zadow asserts her right to be identified as the author of this work in accordance with the Copyright, Designs and Patents Act 1988.

This is a work of fiction. Any resemblance to actual persons, living or dead, is purely coincidental.

All rights reserved. This publication may not be reproduced, stored in a retrieval system or transmitted, in any form or by any means – electronic, mechanical, photocopying, recording or otherwise – without the prior permission of the publisher.

Permission for producing this play may be applied for via the publisher, using the contact details above, or by emailing rights@renardpress.com.

CONTENTS

Fridge	7
Scene One: *My Walls*	11
Scene Two: *Missed Call*	19
Scene Three: *Arrival*	21
Scene Four: *Are You There?*	29
Scene Five: *Sister*	31
Scene Six: *Swellin'*	39
Scene Seven: *Hello Again*	41
Scene Eight: *Now Three*	45
Scene Nine: *Can I Come Out?*	55
Scene Ten: *Friends*	57
Scene Eleven: *Stars*	69
Scene Twelve: *Out*	79
Scene Thirteen: *Stop*	85
Acknowledgements	93

FRIDGE

FOR MY SISTER

CHARACTERS

ALICE
Late-twenties. Originally East Anglian,
but now lives in London.

CHARLIE
Late-twenties/early thirties. ALICE and LO's
childhood friend.

LOIS (LO)
ALICE'S younger sister.

A fridge, whether figurative or literal, should remain
onstage throughout. The fridge acts as bus shelter,
lamp post, TV and seating backing.

SETTING
East Anglia, present.

ACCENTS
Actors should not speak in an exaggerated form
of the East Anglian accent; the dialect should only
be used to inform the casting.

SCENE ONE

My Walls

A fridge stands in darkness. The sound of the countryside can be heard – birds, etc. Slight pause. The fridge suddenly jerks and shakes. Someone is inside.

LO (*from inside the fridge*): Alice! Alice! Let me out! It's not funny any more!

(*The sound of laughs and giggles.*)

It's not funny!

(*A knocking is heard. More shaking, until there is one last jerk. Suddenly, the door swings open and out is thrown* LO. *She falls on to her face. She sits up. She is not used to the light, and her eyes ache. Time has passed. She sees bottles of milkshake in neat lines left for her. She takes a bottle. She opens it with her mouth, tearing the plastic with her teeth and unscrewing the top with ease. She's done this before. She stares at a note in her hand. She crumples it into a ball suddenly. She sits cross-legged. She takes the milkshake bottle and gulps it down in one go. This should be uncomfortable to watch. It dribbles down her neck. She finishes it. She exhales and swigs.*)

FRIDGE

I want to be just like my...

(Shadows stream on the floor. The birdsong slows down to an unnatural slow speed.)

Alice? *(The wind howls.)* When it's this quiet all the time, you can't help but hear voices, right? *(The wind howls louder. She peers under the fridge and squeezes her hand underneath.)* One time, Alice put me in the fridge because she told me the sea tale of the Old Mermaid of Shipden.

This is the true story of a girl
Who was banished underwater.
So her people stopped calling her 'daughter'.
She lived there alone
And above her lost ships would groan;
The sea winds would howl
And the seals would growl
At her shedding tail
Cos she failed.
She wanted to return to the land.
The North Sea raged
As she grew ever more caged.
With hull upon hull
Her collection did grow,
And they sunk to her below.

So, the Shipden mermaid wore
Legs made of wood
From long-gone shipwrecks

SCENE ONE: MY WALLS

To come at last ashore –
To find her family's door
At last. But the folk of old Shipden
Said she hunted for the most beautiful hair
From little human girls.
Then she'd scalp and steal
The hair and wear them in her lair.
But she wore her wooden legs
Of the wrecks
And came to the town,
To the door of the family
That sent her down
To that watery cell.
She knocked and knocked,
But they wouldn't open it.
Pleading, screaming,
Her shriek with a creak
Sent the entire town
To the murky depths.
And she returned to her shell;
There she wept,
Waiting for another door
To knock on
On shore.

So, she went outside when I couldn't. But I think it was just to have a smoke with Chrissy by the guinea-pig hutch.

(*A knock comes from the gloom.*)

She said she fought it with fire. (*She rolls her sleeve up. The wind howls again.*) The winds are stronger here – there's nothing in the way for miles and miles. We put houses in the way of the howls.

(ALICE, *a distortion of a memory. Her voice fades in and out of focus, as per* LO's *conscience. To* LO, ALICE *is present. She appears in a blue light, perhaps. Ghoulish.*)

Alice? (*Slight pause.*) Alice? Alice? Are you there?

(*Pause.*)

ALICE: I'm here. Always have been.

(*Pause.*)

LO: Why didn't you let me out?
ALICE: Don't fall asleep on me.
LO: I'm the Mermaid of Shipden.
ALICE: That wasn't real.
LO: Like you? She stole my hair. I think she did.
ALICE: Now I steal you back! There's a good girl. Look at this.
LO: The world stopped when I—
ALICE: That's enough. I'm going for a smoke.
LO: Can I come with you?
ALICE: No.
LO: Stay with me.
ALICE: Promise. (*Pause.*) No one should see this. This is ours, understand?

SCENE ONE: MY WALLS

LO (*nods*): Are you coming back?
ALICE (*laughs*): Where else would I want to be? (*The blue light disappears with* ALICE.)

(*The wind howls. A knock is heard again.*)

VOICE FROM OUTSIDE: Oi'm hayre!

(LO *panics. She scurries to the fridge and hides something underneath it again, opens it and slams it shut. The milkshake bottles are left alone. A figure enters: tall, wearing a hood against the wind and weather. He carries a large bag over his shoulder. He brings fallen leaves in with him under his workmen's boots.*)

MAN: 'Ello 'un? (*He sees the milkshake bottles and crouches down, inspecting them.*) Looks t' me loike the tracks of a... (*He swings the fridge door open, finding her.* LO *screams.*) What you doin' down in hayre?
LO: In here?
MAN: In hayre.
LO: What you doin' out thayre, Charlie?
CHARLIE: What you doin', oi?

(*She jumps into his arms, wrapping her legs around him like a monkey. We see him properly.* CHARLIE *is a young man, rugged, wearing boots and a fleece – a working man of the countryside. He is young, but a rural working life has left his face aged by the elements.*)

Waho! Chrissy called me, so 'ere oi am.
LO: I wonder if she uses the same room every time...

CHARLIE: Now, now. She is yer mum. (*Slight pause.*) Now, you know what t' do. Just like Alice taught you. (*He swings the bag off his shoulder and on to the floor. He unzips it and waits for* LO.)

LO: Dippers?

CHARLIE: Check.

LO: Fries-2-Go?

CHARLIE: Double check. (LO *looks down.* CHARLIE *points at the empty bottles of milkshake.*) Already?

LO: Sorry.

CHARLIE: Wot yer doin', guzzlin', just loike the Nawfuk pigs in t' field – you be on creep feed!

LO: Oink! Oink!

(*They laugh. He rummages in the bag.*)

Don't forget to do the dippers properly!

CHARLIE: In a circle, roight?

LO: Spiral! Like a snail. That way they get good and crispy at the little tail.

CHARLIE: No they don't—

LO: That's how Alice did them.

CHARLIE: And that's 'ow we'll do them, too.

LO: Mum got me strawberry and not...

BOTH: ...banana...

CHARLIE: I know. You'll make yourself sick by doin' that. Roight. Spar's still open. (*He turns to leave.*)

LO: Charlie?

CHARLIE: Uhuh?

LO: Out there, in the fields, when you're with your drift—

CHARLIE: Made good work of them.

SCENE ONE: MY WALLS

LO: Yeah, but when you are, and if, say one of 'em gets sick, like really sick, really really gross sick, what do you do?

CHARLIE: Well, that would all depend on whether it were a gilt or farrowed yet, or a hog or a boar, but oi'd with all moi power try to get 'em back. They're moi loiveli'ood and—

LO: But if they were so bad—

CHARLIE: Loike if they gots the foot 'n' mouth?

LO: Yeah.

CHARLIE: Oi'd 'ave to burn 'em. To save the drift.

(*Slight pause.*)

LO: You'll miss the Spar! And you're trailing mud into the house! (*He zips his hood up tight.*)

CHARLIE: That never stopped yer sister! (*He exits.*)

(*She checks he's gone. The wind howls again.* LO *crawls to the fridge. She takes a mobile phone from her pocket and dials a number. She reaches back under the fridge and retrieves a hidden object, which she puts in her pocket.*)

LO: I'm just... calling to...

(ALICE *appears again as before.*)

Are you still out there?

(*The following becomes more and more distorted.*)

17

ALICE: Family are the ones who take care of you.

LO: They are the ones you call and call and call and call again because you know that they'll answer.

ALICE: It's not a case of muscle and matter holding you together.

LO: When you reach out their fingers will brush and cradle you, long past the midnight door.

(ALICE *disappears again.* LO *rolls up her sleeves and gets back inside the fridge. She closes the door. Darkness. Perhaps a spotlight on the fridge. We hear her scream.*)

VOICE FROM OUTSIDE: If you would like to re-record your message, press one. To save the message, press two. To listen to this message again, press three… (*Fade out as the wind howls.*)

(*Darkness.*)

SCENE TWO

Missed Call

ALICE *walks rapidly and takes her mobile phone out. A shaky spotlight against the dark, perhaps, follows her. She dials a number. The empty space around her is telling. She slams the fridge out of frustration.* LO, *ghoulish now, crawls out and watches her.*

ALICE: Charlie, I don't know if you'll get this, but I'm getting the train up. I've had voicemails from Lo. What's going on? What's happened? Look, they've called the platform. I'll get the bus as far as I can. Heydon, probably. Anyway, let me know and I'll keep you updated. Oh, and, um, it'll be good to see you again. Yeah... No. That's it.

(*She exits into the darkness.* CHARLIE *appears from the gloom. The same as* ALICE *before – he steps into the same shaky light that followed her. He listens to the voicemail.*)

CHARLIE: Shit. (*His phone rings.*) Uhuh. Eeeyeah... nooo, I know, Mrs Perry-Warnes, it's upsetting you... well, oi thenk you should call someone loike the police if yer that worried... Yeah, I remember your History class... no. No, I didn't mean for that to happen... Mrs... you can't hold that against me for ever...! Will do. Listen, if there's teenagers smoking somethen' outside yer house, what am oi suppos'd t' do 'bout et...? Alroight, but thes is the last toime...! (*He hangs up.*) 'Ere we fucking go.

(*He disappears into the darkness as well.* LO *follows.*)

SCENE THREE

Arrival

Darkness, except for the fridge. ALICE *is put together in a shambolic but coherent fashion – white shirt, unironed, flats not pumps. She checks her phone. There is no signal. She tuts. Paces up and down. Squinting, she shines the light on her phone around to see.*

ALICE: Times, times, times… (*She takes out a cigarette, lights it and leans against the bus shelter.*) I am so fucking tired. (*Cigarette in mouth,* ALICE *looks for the road. Her light flashes across* LO*'s face. She jumps in fear, then looks back again.* LO *is gone.*) For… OK. Alice, you should know these roads. Oh god. I need to find the house. (*She stubs the cigarette out and leans back against the shelter.*)

CHARLIE: 'i! Oi, you en thayre! Best get home, eh, 'fore Mrs Perry-Warnes comes out. Oi won't say a blab. (*Slight pause.*) Foine.

(ALICE *stirs a little.* CHARLIE *comes closer and recognises* ALICE. *She, startled, quickly puts on sunglasses. He pretends not to know her.*)

Urgh. City wankers, eh? Think they can just turn up, build, smoke wherever they please… well, good luck to yer – full of piss in there, anyway!

(ALICE *jumps up, sunglasses still on. She squeals as she recognises* CHARLIE.)

ALICE: I knew it! I knew that wasn't just the smell of horse piss or sheep piss or…
CHARLIE: You weren't asleep after a little… (*He indicates smoking weed with a hand gesture.*)
ALICE: No! God… I need some, though! You got any?
CHARLIE: No… so you weren't—
ALICE: How could I have slept on that all night? I was pretending with this in my hand. (*She pulls out a can of hairspray from her pocket.*)
CHARLIE: That's not pepper spray – that's just a travel-size bottle of hairspray. I may not be from London, but I'm not an idiot.
ALICE: Yeah, I know – still has the same effect though. And I'm not a London wanker. I'm *from* here.
CHARLIE: You bloody well ain't. Everyone round here knows there's no point getting the bus – never turns up on match day… or after three – buses stop at three.
ALICE: How could I forget that! Well, I haven't been round here for a while.

(ALICE *adjusts her glasses to cover her eyes completely, then rummages in her pockets for her cigarettes; hastily she pats herself down, still not finding them. She quickens her search. A frenzy of addiction.*)

CHARLIE: You all right? You havin' a fit or something? Cos I'm not really first-aid trained. Well I am, but only for horses and cows… Not sheep though. Can't do sheep.

SCENE THREE: ARRIVAL

ALICE: What? No. Yes. No. I'll go into a fit if I don't find... (ALICE *recovers the pack from her inner coat pocket, which she had left lying on the bench.*) Aha!

(ALICE *triumphantly waves the cigarettes in his face; he grimaces. She lights one and slumps back on the grass; she exhales with relief.*)

CHARLIE: Should have known you'd be on them, from London and all.

ALICE: If you don't like it, you can get back to your cow first-aid training.

CHARLIE: I don't *teach* the cows first-aid training. And I can do horses too.

ALICE: I do know you can't teach cows first aid. They're built to fall over, anyway, so why do they need first aid from you?

CHARLIE: You said you're from around here.

ALICE: Was.

CHARLIE: Was. Roight.

ALICE (*she smirks, knowingly*): You went to the local comp, right?

CHARLIE: Oi did, yeah.

ALICE: So did I.

CHARLIE: Wait. You went here? Did you... did you know Mrs Perry-Warnes?

ALICE: So old everyone joked she'd lived through *everything* that she taught us in History.

CHARLIE: That's roight! You see that there cottage?

ALICE: Yeah.

CHARLIE: That's hers.

ALICE: No way!

FRIDGE

CHARLIE: Uhuh. Shacked up with three greyhounds named after her ex-husbands. Um, Mike, Benny and…

CHARLIE AND ALICE: Whitney! (*They laugh together.*)

(CHARLIE *reaches for her sunglasses; she tries to pull away, but he grabs them off her face. All pretence is dropped.*)

ALICE: I've changed a lot since I dated Rob.

CHARLIE: Oi dunno 'bout that.

ALICE: You still best mates?

CHARLIE: Um, no, not really – lost contact after he went into the army. Oi got your voicemail. Bad signal, though, 'round 'ere.

ALICE: How could I forget?

CHARLIE: Figured you were the mystery weed smoker after Perry-Warnes called me.

ALICE: She did?

CHARLIE: Tends to these days. Oi'm more reliable than the Neighbourhood Watch helpline.

ALICE: You always were. (*Slight pause.*) I tried to get closer to the house but—

CHARLIE: It's OK. You never learnt to drive, you twat.

(ALICE *crosses her arms and looks at the bus shelter.*)

Memories, eh?

ALICE: Something like that.

CHARLIE: Thought you and Rob would last for ever. (*Slight pause.*) You shouldn't smoke those anyway.

ALICE: Why?

CHARLIE: Because they kill you.

SCENE THREE: ARRIVAL

(LO *watches the fridge as if it is a TV.*)

ALICE: Why?
CHARLIE: Because they fill your lungs up with tar and you can't breathe.
ALICE: Why?
CHARLIE: Because… because—
ALICE: You've gone rusty.
CHARLIE: Because… well, they kill you, don't they?
ALICE: Lions can kill you, but we still try to tame them.

(*Pause.*)

CHARLIE (*gesturing at her shoes*): They won't stay clean long.
ALICE (*shrugging*): Work stuff.
CHARLIE: Right… I know I shouldn't be saying this…
ALICE: Then why are you?
CHARLIE: Well. What I wanted to say is, I'm sorry about Lo.
ALICE: What makes you so interested?
CHARLIE: I was… I have been… I mean, when she needs someone to… be there… Y'know?

(*Slight pause.*)

ALICE: No. I don't.
CHARLIE: Alroight! Alroight! Still snarky as ever.
ALICE: Still smelly as ever.

(*Pause. They stare out at the fields in front of them.*)

CHARLIE: Your hair – it's different. It's pretty. I like it. It used to be bright blonde, like Alice in Wonderland. But I like it now.

LO: That was the 1959 one, which combined both books. It didn't have the knights in it, though.

ALICE: Really?

CHARLIE: Yeah. (ALICE *looks at him.*) I can read, you know.

ALICE: And who do I remind you of now?

CHARLIE: I dunno. It's just a book. Ain't gonna change me. (CHARLIE *sits down next to her.* ALICE *offers him a drag.*) No. No, thank you. I'm not a—

ALICE: —city wanker? (CHARLIE *shrugs.* ALICE *sees him eye up the cigarette as she puts it to her mouth.*) You used to.

(CHARLIE *eventually reaches for it and takes one long, slow drag. Exhales.*)

Just like old times. Complete with the shitty bus shelter. I can't believe this thing is still here.

CHARLIE: Don't you think we should get to your house? Lo's probably waiting, and—

ALICE: I mean, even this bus shelter – this shitty piss-filled bus shelter. The stories we could tell! To everyone else it's a failure of public transport on the county council's behalf, but to us every bit of graffiti is a chapter in the chronicles of four teens marooned in the countryside.

CHARLIE (*pointing*): There's a badly proportioned penis.

ALICE (*turns to look under the seat and reads*): 'Charlie was here.' Original. (*Looks again.*) Oh yeah. Is that life-size or to scale? Maybe it's the angle you drew it…

SCENE THREE: ARRIVAL

CHARLIE: I don't think I thought much about scale back then.

ALICE: There's more! (*Reads:*) 'Rob and Alice 4EVA.'

LO: The end.

CHARLIE: Not quoite for ever, was it?

ALICE: Not even close.

CHARLIE: Five minutes feels like for ever when you're fifteen.

(*They look into each other. Pause.*)

It's good to see you.

ALICE: You too.

CHARLIE: Oi just wish it were under better—

ALICE: Stop. We know the circumstances.

(LO *gestures with a remote at the fridge, as though turning a TV off.*)

CHARLIE: I could give you a lift, if you want, to your house – my car is parked at the top of the road.

ALICE: No thanks.

CHARLIE: Oh.

ALICE: I just want to walk. Fresh air and all that.

CHARLIE: With that? (*Indicates cigarette.*)

ALICE: I need to counter all this nature with some kind of pollution. All this green – not natural, is it?

CHARLIE: You're city-wankering on me again, Alice.

ALICE: Whoops.

CHARLIE: Maybe I'll see you around or something?

ALICE: That could be... nice.

CHARLIE: Nice? (*Slightly repulsed.*) Well, it was *nice* talking to you, Alice.

FRIDGE

ALICE: Anyway, best get on polluting the English countryside.

CHARLIE: Mind Neighbourhood Watch don't catch you.

ALICE: Nah, it's the National Trust I've got to worry about. (*She looks slightly embarrassed.*)

(CHARLIE *looks at her. She looks at the graffiti on the bus shelter again.*)

CHARLIE: OK. (CHARLIE *gets up to leave. He remembers* LO. *He turns.*) Aren't you going to go now? It'll take you...

ALICE: Charlie?

CHARLIE: Yeah?

(*His fear and concern shows. Her face drops.*)

ALICE: Tell me straight. What exactly has been going on?

CHARLIE: Alice, oi—

ALICE: I don't need you to be nice to me now... I need to know how much of her is left.

(*Silence.*)

CHARLIE: I'll drop you off.

(*They exit.* LO *remains on stage during the following transition.*)

28

FRIDGE

(ALICE *looks at her.* LO *fixes her stare on* ALICE. *It freezes her.*)

I'm going to bed.

(ALICE *doesn't respond, and just watches her leave. She looks back at the sky where* LO *was looking before.*)

ALICE: Melt me down
    And mould me
    For the trophy
    On the mantle
    Of many.
    I'm sat above the roar of the fire
    And my bones golden to a mass
    Of wanton dreams.

(ALICE *goes inside.*)

SCENE FOUR

Are You There?

ALICE *and* LO's *garden.* LO *looks out over the landscape, up at the sky and night air.* ALICE *runs in, breathless.* LO *stands. She doesn't turn to see her sister.* ALICE *heaves and smiles.* LO *looks at her, expressionless, coldly.*

ALICE: I'm here!

(LO *doesn't react. She continues to look up at the sky.* ALICE *goes towards her and stands next to her.*)

What are you doing out here?

(*Slight pause.* ALICE *is still heaving and is cle[arly waiting for a] response.*)

LO: I got out.
ALICE: What?
LO: Of the fridge.
ALICE: What?
LO: That's what you

SCENE FIVE

Sister

ALICE *and* LO*'s house, inside. Morning.* LO *is in front of the TV again, which lights up her face; otherwise there is darkness.* ALICE *enters, carrying a box of CDs and mementos. She is beaming with positivity at a new day.* LO *is conscious of everything* ALICE *is doing, but she continues to watch the TV.*

LO: What's all that?

ALICE (*trying to make conversation*): Well, I was going through my old room and found all this stuff! Thought it would be embarrassing.

LO: No one goes in there any more.

ALICE: Hey, all this was from when I was a kid – I was a real 90s kid.

LO: I was born in the 90s too!

ALICE: But you don't remember anything! You were born in '97, for god's sake. I'm a '90s kid' because I remember it…

LO: I still count. There's a nine in '97.

ALICE: But you don't remember anything from the 90s! (*Pause.*) I'm trying my best here, and the least you—

LO: Shut up.

FRIDGE

(ALICE *is silent.*)

You never came back. (*Pause.* LO *watches TV.*) Do you know about Rob?
ALICE: What happened?
LO: Last I knew, he was flying out for his last tour with the reg.
ALICE: When was that?
LO: Two years ago.
ALICE: Nothing since?
LO: Nope. Didn't Charlie tell you? (*Slight pause.*) Nice choker. You wear that when you were five?
ALICE: Seven, actually…

(ALICE *removes the choker sheepishly and puts a disc in a CD player.*)

LO: Isn't that S Club 7?
ALICE: Well, you recognised it, so… (ALICE *carries the CD player flat to keep it playing. She tries to distract* LO *from the TV.*) Wait. Wait wait wait wait. This is… hang on, it's got to go around to the chorus. Wait!

(ALICE *moves to the music; a 90s tune can be heard playing on her headphones. She keeps the CD player flat on her palm to keep it playing. She dances the routine with precision and pride.*)

LO: Typical.
ALICE: I'm trying here! I took time off work to be here, you know.
LO: I'm trying to watch this. It's the best part.

SCENE FIVE: SISTER

(*The TV turns blue.* ALICE *dances.*)

ALICE: Oh come on, you know our dance routine to this!
LO: *Your* dance routine, you mean.
ALICE: Reach for the—
LO: I SAID NO.

(ALICE *stops. The CD player skips.*)

ALICE: Dammit. If you don't keep it flat, it messes the song up.

(LO *gives up and goes over to* ALICE.)

LO: And it went like this.

(*She dances the routine perfectly, expressionless.*)

ALICE: Oh, wow…! (*She now seems encouraged by* LO *and continues with the nostalgic conversation.*) Do you remember dial-up? There was that stupid noise it used to make, wasn't there! How'd it go?

(ALICE *impersonates the dial up sound.* LO *joins her in making the sound. They laugh together.*)

LO: Drove Mum mad.
ALICE: Where's she this time?

(LO *scurries back to the TV, and is again engrossed. Cross-legged.*)

FRIDGE

LO: Went to Ibiza with the latest.
ALICE: John the architect?
LO: No.
ALICE: John the dermatologist?
LO: No.
ALICE: John the estate agent?
LO: No. (*Slight pause.*) Harry the asshole.
ALICE: Oh. Haven't met that one. How long?
LO: Coupla months.
ALICE: When do they get back?
LO: They left a week ago.
ALICE: You've been here for a week?
LO: I can look after myself.
ALICE: Clearly.
LO: Whatever.

(*Pause.*)

ALICE: I met Charlie at the bus stop on the way here. He dropped me off.
LO: Great.
ALICE: Yeah.
LO: Is that why you were weird?
ALICE: What? It wasn't weird… it was just… nice.
LO: Just nice?
ALICE: Yeah.
LO: OK…
ALICE: Oh, shut up.

(*They smirk together warmly. Silence.*)

How are we going to do this then?

SCENE FIVE: SISTER

LO: You sound 'proactive', Little Miss Employee of the Month.
ALICE: You know we need to talk about it.
LO: What d'ya mean?
ALICE: Never mind.

(*Long pause.*)

LO: I want to go see the orang-utans somewhere like Thailand or Borneo. I want to see a wild one in its home for the last time, before it's all destroyed... the forest, I mean. Can you do something for me?
ALICE: Um, sure.
LO: Can you get me a milkshake? They're over there—
ALICE: All right.
LO: You remember.

(ALICE *goes and gets one and returns with it to* LO, *who is still in front of the TV.* LO *takes it.*)

Thank you. You can have one if you want. (*She opens it the same way as before.*)
ALICE: You learnt well... (LO *looks at her.*) So... Are we going to do this – talk about it? Help me here, I'm not very good at doing this. You've got to give me something to work with – what about, I don't know... the... (*searches for words*) run-up? Is that what you call it? Running up to it?

(*Pause.* LO *glugs a little.*)

FRIDGE

And where was Mum during all of this? Jesus, when I started this new job, I thought you'd be able to deal with some things on your own. Where was she? Where was she? You, upstairs, her downstairs? Did she have someone downstairs? Did she drown you out? Or did you drown her out? Oh shit, I'm sorry. I didn't mean to... Did you use mine? It couldn't be, unless it was all rusted up. Could have got an infection if you did, using a rusty razor... Although you probably weren't worrying about getting an infection when you wouldn't be... Oh shit. What am I talking about?

(*Pause.*)

LO: Six years since you looked in that box. (*She watches the TV still, glugging as she goes. The* Blue Planet *soundtrack or similar begins to play.*) I saw this documentary with David Attenborough – I'd been following it for weeks, through the African savannah, to the polar ice caps, across the Pacific; his voice travelled over all this life, all this land, and it was all in front of me, every week. I waited till the sixth week. Borneo. Jungle. Miles and miles of jungle. Deep. Dark. Wet. Throbbing. Thriving. And I feel weird saying this, but I *felt* the jungle – I felt its mystery, its green emptiness and fullness, all at the same time, and I wasn't even there – I was just sitting in this house drinking fucking tea. And then, out of it all, out of the depths of this emptiness, wading through the undergrowth was an orang-utan, with the smallest,

SCENE FIVE: SISTER

smallest little thing on her back. Grabbing and holding on to her so tightly. Her and this tiny little baby orang-utan were just wandering through this jungle in Borneo, glowing in all that green, searching for food, shelter... another orang-utan? I dunno. David was giving me facts about the ecosystem, and above him, above that voice, the voice that says 'nature', that little orang-utan on its mother's back turned to me, looked into me – it looked *into* me. They were looking for me, they were wandering alone through the jungle, through miles of the stuff, and this tiny little thing found me in this house, with my tea and with no one to hold on to. It found me, Alice. I lost you. But it found me. It found me here. (*Pause.*) I hate this place.

ALICE: I know. (*She looks at* LO.) Would you just... would you just look at me?

(LO*'s eyes are wet.*)

37

SCENE SIX

Swellin'

Outside, on the land. CHARLIE *enters with a bucket. He pours out feed for the 'sow' in front of him.*

CHARLIE: There you go, girl. Help you grow big and strong. We want tha'. You've got a good farrow going on, ha'n't you? Nestin' means you're soon. (*He smiles.*) I know. I know it hurts. But not long now… Charlie'll take care of yer… Like he's done before. (*He gets up and picks up the bucket. He empties out the last few bits from the bottom. He turns to find* LO *watching him. Pause.*) You're outside!
LO: She's there.
CHARLIE: Ah.

(*Slight pause.*)

LO: I'm scared. (*Slight pause.*) You don't get scared.
CHARLIE: Yeah, I do.
LO: How?
CHARLIE: Even us out here get scared. (*He strokes the sow.*) It's what's inside when we go home that's scarier.

(*He gestures for her to join him. She does. They kneel together. Pause.*)

LO (*hesitantly putting her hand on the sow's belly*): It tickles.
CHARLIE: She's nestin'.
LO: For how long?
CHARLIE: Until it's the roight time to have 'em comin'.
LO: You mean, she's—
CHARLIE: —pregnant, yeah. Her first. Oi's got a good feelen' 'bout this litter.
LO: How do you know?
CHARLIE: I just feel et. You get a feelen' 'bout these things.

(*Pause.*)

LO: I could be my sister. I could.

(CHARLIE *remains silent. She leans her head on his shoulder. Slight pause.* CHARLIE *stands up suddenly.*)

CHARLIE: She's swellin' somethin' sore. Needs rest.

(LO *stands. They look at each other.*)

But it's good to have her out in the open air. With that low sun, she'll perk up.
LO: You've taken good care of her.
CHARLIE: Just a little whoile more. It's a very... delicate toime. Gotta be careful.

(*Pause.*)

LO (*squinting*): That low sun is really bright.
CHARLIE: It happens in summer.

(*He exits in a hurry.* LO *is left looking at the sow.*)

SCENE SEVEN

Hello Again

Two days later: the bus shelter. ALICE *is sitting, and has lollipops. Waiting for* CHARLIE. *He enters, rattled.*

ALICE: You alroight?
CHARLIE: One of the sows' got a babe in its belly! This is… it's really… it's a very delicate toime. Gonna be a good'n. Oi can feel et.
ALICE: That's great, Charlie.
CHARLIE: Yeah, oi got a real good feelin' 'bout this one.
ALICE: How long?
CHARLIE: We can't tell gestation just yet – she's always been huge! (ALICE *offers her lollipop to him.*) Don't be disgustin'!
ALICE: What's wrong with it?
CHARLIE: Oi don't want 'girl disease' do oi? (ALICE *laughs. She gives him his own. He sucks on it with glee and then lifts it.*) To the baba in moi sow!

(ALICE *motions 'cheers' with her lollipop. They suck on their own lollipops. Pause.*)

ALICE: Why didn't this kill us back then?
CHARLIE: 'Back then'? it was six years ago, Alice, not a lifetime!

(ALICE *looks at her lollipop.*)

ALICE: I don't know why I'm eating this. It's too sweet for me now.
CHARLIE: Lo loikes 'em.
ALICE: Can't stop her.
CHARLIE: Yep. Down the hatch loike moi gilts, she is.
ALICE: She hasn't changed. At all.
CHARLIE: It's hard to here.
ALICE (*dips her lollipop in sugar dust, which goes all over her face*): I mean, do you think I've changed?
CHARLIE (*smiles*): No.

(CHARLIE *indicates with his own lip the sugar dust on hers.* ALICE *reaches with her tongue to lick it off, but can't reach it, so wipes it off with her sleeve instead.*)

Alice?
ALICE: Hmm?
CHARLIE: Nothing.

(*Slight pause.*)

ALICE: Charlie, I need you to help me.
CHARLIE: OK.
ALICE: You should have told me about Chrissy going off with—

SCENE SEVEN: HELLO AGAIN

CHARLIE: Harry the arsehole.
ALICE: Right. Him.
CHARLIE: Yeah, but it weren't really moi bizness, was et?
ALICE: I know you knew.
CHARLIE (*huffs*): Oi've done moi bit. Got moi own, too.
ALICE: Is that what you've got?
CHARLIE: She's your sister.
ALICE: Don't you blame me!
CHARLIE: I'm part of this family, so whoi not?
ALICE: You should have told me!
CHARLIE: We don't talk any more, Alice!

(*Pause.*)

ALICE: You could have called!
LO: No one just calls!

(*Slight pause.*)

CHARLIE (*gingerly*): Do you want to… you can say no, it's fine, but do you… would you want to come around tonight?
ALICE: If you knew her like I do you'd understand. (*Slight pause.*) I'm not planning to date or anything…
CHARLIE (*laughing nervously*): I meant just as friends. You know? It's a bit rough and weird and… (*Suddenly:*) It's a day to celebrate, after all, with the new one on the way. It'd be cool—
ALICE: If you get bourbons I'm there, then.
CHARLIE: Great. Cool. Um, I'll see you there, then.
ALICE: Yeah. (*Slight pause.*) Bye then.

FRIDGE

CHARLIE: Yeah. (ALICE *turns to exit and he thinks she's left.*) YES! (ALICE, *having seen* CHARLIE, *returns.* CHARLIE *quickly turns.*) Yes?

ALICE: We should see how Lo is. No sharp objects and all.

(CHARLIE *laughs out of politeness.*)

That wasn't a joke.

(*He stops.*)

CHARLIE: I know. I was just laughing cos...
ALICE: Cos?
CHARLIE (*nervously*): Oi dunno.

(*Slight pause.*)

ALICE: OK...
CHARLIE: Um, yeah, but I think you should know that oi've actually been—
ALICE: Uhuh?
CHARLIE: Nothing.
ALICE (*smirks*): OK... Come on, then. Oh, and Charlie?
CHARLIE: Yes?
ALICE: It's always best to check the girl has left before celebrating.

(CHARLIE *nods. They leave.*)

SCENE EIGHT

Now Three

ALICE, LO *and* CHARLIE *are in the sisters' living room. Daytime. All three are watching the TV, which blares at them. Something like Disney music swells in a distorted manner. This should feel uneasy, and the TV screen should flicker and jolt violently.*

ALICE: Lo, when oi invited Charlie round I thought we'd…
LO: Sshhh!
CHARLIE (*whispering*): It's OK. Really.
ALICE: No, it's not. Lo!
CHARLIE: It's really—
LO: Quiet! This is the bit where he finds her!
CHARLIE: I've seen this before, so it's not a big—
ALICE: You have?
LO: Would you two shut up!
CHARLIE: I meant, it's her favourite bit.
LO: Charlie's here after the sow-feeding. Always after feeding the fat heif with the belly.
CHARLIE: Oi think she means before… it's happened before, roight, Lo?
LO: Right.
ALICE: Oh.

(The music swells louder for the ending. Operatic and loud. They sit for a moment. ALICE *gets up and turns the lights on.)*

That's enough. *(Slight pause.)* You've got to stop. *(She goes over to* LO *and tries to force her to get up.)* This can't be helping your—
CHARLIE: I'm not sure that's the best way—
ALICE *(she turns viciously, turning the TV off swiftly)*: She's my sister!
CHARLIE *(retreating)*: But, you know, your way seems good too.
LO *(fighting* ALICE*)*: Don't touch me! Get away from us! *(*LO *directs a fierce look at* ALICE. ALICE *lets go.)*
CHARLIE: Oh, come on. You can't say that.
ALICE: They're only stories. They're not real. Nothing like that happens here.
LO: Not to people like you! Just look at you!

*(*ALICE *controls herself coolly.)*

CHARLIE: Sisters, eh?

*(*ALICE *and* LO *both glower at him. Pause.)*

Great! Now, if you want to talk evil, I can go on about the match-day traffic till, well, till you shut me up. Because that truly is pure evil.
LO: Charlie gets it.
CHARLIE: Do oi? Well, um, they made me feel like oi could be anything.

*(*LO *rolls her eyes.)*

SCENE EIGHT: NOW THREE

LO: You're a farmer with a big fat pregnant pig, and that is the most interesting thing about you.

(CHARLIE *shuffles uncomfortably.*)

CHARLIE: I'm here. that's gotta mean something.
LO: Ah, yes. But for how long?
ALICE: This isn't healthy.
LO: What are you trying to say, Alice?

(ALICE *goes to the door.*)

That's it. Go when it gets complicated!
ALICE: Oh god. Here we go.
LO: Something you'd like to share with the group?
ALICE: It's like you don't want anyone to be happy if you're not.
LO: Don't tell me Disney is a prescription drug for twenty-something depression.
ALICE: No, I'm not saying that. And I'm not the one who's d… d…
LO: Oh my god, she can't even say it.
ALICE: Are you enjoying this?
LO: Go on.
CHARLIE: She's right. This isn't helping anyone.
LO: Really? But I think she's just like me – d… d…
ALICE: I'm nothing like you.
LO: Y'think? You're single. You're in denial. You hate your job. You hate your family. And you live in… where is it, again?
ALICE: Sidcup.

47

FRIDGE

LO: Case closed. You're depressed.
ALICE: *You're* depressed!
LO: You are!
ALICE: Says you! You know, you've always been—
CHARLIE: ALROIGHT! Alroight, alroight. There. We're all depressed. Happy now?

(*Slight pause.*)

LO: Charlie, you're not.
CHARLIE: Why can't I be? I could be.
LO: We all know *I* am... I think you've been watching too much TV. Remember what your mum said about square eyes...

(ALICE *smirks.*)

ALICE: The NHS will have queues of 90s kids with the condition.
LO: Popping pills all over again.
CHARLIE: Popping over Poppins.

(*He laughs hysterically and nudges* LO, *who recoils; then an idea comes to her and she nudges him back.*)

LO: She likes you.
CHARLIE: That's not true. Wait, what?
LO: She hasn't corrected me yet, so—
ALICE: Jesus. Are you trying to turn everything into an argument?
CHARLIE: Is it?
ALICE: No!

SCENE EIGHT: NOW THREE

(*Pause.*)

CHARLIE: I'd better go.
ALICE: That was cruel.
LO: He's a big man. He can take care of himself.
CHARLIE: I'm really going to go…
ALICE: No, stay!
LO: That's what Charlie does best. Stay, Charlie.
ALICE: Don't talk to him like that.
LO: Like what? Like I'm breaking his heart? Like you just did?

(ALICE *contains herself.*)

ALICE: I'm not doing this with you. Come on, Charlie.

(*She moves towards the door.*)

CHARLIE: I don't think this is really about me any more…
    (*He goes towards the door and gets there before* ALICE *does.*)
LO: You stay.
ALICE: Don't talk to him like that!
LO: What? Like you did ten years ago?
ALICE: You remember a lot of things differently.

(*Silence.*)

LO: Charlie knows his way around here, don't you?
CHARLIE: Stop it.

(LO *wanders over to the fridge. She plays with the magnets on the door.*)

ALICE: What the fuck is wrong with you?

FRIDGE

LO: *No-stal-gi-a.* Weird word isn't it? Supposed to be Latin or something. Can't remember now.
CHARLIE: It's Greek.

(*They look at him.*)

LO: I'm tired.
ALICE: Now, Lo…
LO: LEAVE! YOU LEFT ME HERE, SO GO!
CHARLIE: Lo…
LO: What, Charlie? What? You gonna take care of me now that she's back?
ALICE: What's she talking about?
LO: He's been here, like I said.
ALICE: Yes, I know.
LO: No. He's been here the whole time.
ALICE: Charlie?

(*Pause.*)

LO: Oh! He hasn't said yet? Too busy getting excited about his little gilt popping one out in the mud?
ALICE: He's only just got here.
LO: Chivalrous and modest.
ALICE: Charlie?
CHARLIE: Look. She's roight. But only cos you went, and then Chrissy's been… indisposed.
LO: Long word there.
ALICE: Shut up!
CHARLIE: Steady on! Alice, it's not what—
LO: See. He doesn't want it coming out.
ALICE: Charlie?
CHARLIE: It's nothing. I mean, not nothing, I've been—

SCENE EIGHT: NOW THREE

ALICE: Oh my god.
CHARLIE: No no no no no no. It's not like... she's very—
LO: —sick?
CHARLIE: Yes!
ALICE: What?
CHARLIE: I mean no! I mean... oh god.
ALICE: Someone tell me what's been going on!
CHARLIE: Oi... oi didn't want to tell you cos oi thought it would make you feel like shit.
LO: He's been with me because he couldn't be with you.
ALICE: Why do you have to be so crazy?

(LO *freezes.*)

CHARLIE: Alice, you can't say things like—
ALICE: Oh, why not? She's got away with talking like that long enough.
CHARLIE: Listen to me! I have been here. But not like that. That's the truth.

(*Pause.*)

ALICE (*to* LO): Is it?

(LO *nods.*)

> So, my best friend has been taking care of my sister and not telling me.

(*Slight pause.*)

CHARLIE: I'm not really your best friend any more, am oi? We haven't been for a whoile.

FRIDGE

LO: That's true. Anyway, he's *my* best friend now.
CHARLIE: She needed help and—
ALICE: I wasn't here. I get it.
LO: You didn't say goodbye! And you know what? I expected a fridge-magnet message at least, I really did.
ALICE: You love those things.
LO: Yeah, I did. And I loved *you*. Why'd you go when there was someone here that loved you? Why, Alice? WHY?
ALICE: Because you needed to know what it felt like.
LO: TO WHAT?
ALICE: TO BE ME!

(*Silence.*)

LO: Well, you can just leave all over again, can't you! I'm sure you'll have no scars on your conscience a second time. I'M SURE I'LL COPE WITHOUT YOU – I MEAN, LOOK HOW I'M DOING RIGHT NOW! I'M JUST DOING JUST GREAT! I'm the runt of the litter, Charlie.
CHARLIE: Remember what we said, Lo? About the drift? We've gotta save what we have left.
LO (*to* ALICE): You think running away from here would stop you turning into Chrissy? You ran, and you've become worse than her!

(ALICE *rises, and approaches* LO *viciously, not thinking.*)

CHARLIE: Alice! She doesn't mean it!

(*She stops herself.*)

LO: You should listen to us.
CHARLIE: Not helping!

SCENE EIGHT: NOW THREE

ALICE: Apologise!
LO: No.
ALICE: Why would you lie about something like that?
CHARLIE: I think we should all just take a step—
LO: Stop trying to be my sister again!
ALICE: I don't have a choice! (*She turns to exit.*)
LO: Wow. Thanks.
CHARLIE: Lo could you just, please—
ALICE: Stop playing the good guy and trying to make it better!
LO: You've come back here and you think we're just going to let you in? Like that?
ALICE: It's not going to get better between us! You're not family, Charlie!

(*Pause.*)

CHARLIE: Oi've gotta get back to the drift. Sow needs feedin'.

(*Silence. He goes to the TV and flicks it on.* LO *runs to it automatically, and her mood swiftly changes into excitement.*)

She'll want another milkshake. Banana.
ALICE: I know.
CHARLIE: Yes. Well, you know her better than me.
LO: Shh!
CHARLIE: I'll see you later.

(CHARLIE *exits.* ALICE *watches* LO *from afar. Silence.*)

LO (*to the TV*): Tell him!

FRIDGE

ALICE (*running to her and slapping her around the face*): Snap out of it!

(LO *remains watching the TV, unfeeling and ignoring* ALICE. ALICE *shakes her. No response.*)

LO: That's new.
ALICE: What's wrong with you?
LO: I really felt like we were getting somewhere there.
ALICE: You want your own world? You can have it! Just don't expect me to come running when you get stuck in… that fridge again. (*Slight pause.*) I can't believe you're my sister.
LO: I wish I was adopted.
ALICE: So do I.

(*She turns to exit.* LO *is still staring at the TV.*)

LO: I'll do it this time.

(ALICE *starts to leave.*)

Where are you going?
ALICE: Charlie and I need to talk.
LO: You watch the TV like a good girl whilst Mummy and Daddy talk in the other room.
ALICE: Well, you can have a think about what you've done, then, can't you? (*She goes to exit.*)
LO: As soon as you leave, I will… I promise.
ALICE: Good. Then I won't ever have to come back here again.

(*She exits.* LO *is left alone.*)

SCENE NINE

Can I Come Out?

Continuous. The fridge blares blue. LO *looks at it and opens a milkshake bottle. Perhaps a spotlight, as before, on* LO. *The space becomes dark, as before.*

LO: Once upon a time,
    In a land flat, flat away…
    No – far, far away…
    There lived a…
    And there were
    Monsters and knives
    And teen brides riddlin' their lives.
    And a hero strives
    But the Sea Witch blinds.

    …

    I know she sees scarred
    eyes. Scarred nightmares too.
    I know you do.

(*She slurps. Out of the darkness,* ALICE *moves through the space, in and out of the light. She is on the phone, battling against the wind.*)

FRIDGE

ALICE: Hello? I said it won't take long... no, honestly... Hello? It's the wind here – it rolls straight off the sea... I said straight off the... never mind...! I'll be back on Monday... just family stuff... nothing... I said... it's not important... I'll be there!

(*She staggers through the wind, out of the light, which flickers.*)

LO: Alice, can I have a hug? Alice? Hello? (*She smiles and slurps harder.*) Make it stop! Make it all stop!

(ALICE *appears again in the flickering light.*)

ALICE (*continuing, on the phone*): I told you... I need to get back there... it's a lost... the winds blow harder here. It's fucking freezing...! I said *freezing*! (*Turning to* LO:) Serotonin's a bitch, darling. Eat up.

(LO *slurps harder.*)

Daddy's little girl. Sister's little problem. Mum's little mistake.

(ALICE *disappears.*)

LO: Hello? Hello? (LO *crawls towards the fridge, helplessly unhinges the door, climbs inside and holds her knees up to her chin.*) Alice? (*From inside the fridge:*) Alice, I'm sorry. Can I come out now?

(*Darkness.*)

SCENE TEN

Friends

The lights come up on CHARLIE*'s living room.* ALICE *knocks on the door furiously.* CHARLIE *looks and sees her. He mouths 'Shit'. During the following the fridge jerks, with* LO *kicking inside.*

ALICE: Charlie!
CHARLIE (*sing-song*): Just a minute!
ALICE: Let me in! We need to talk about—
CHARLIE: Yep, sure, just wait a sec!

(*He busies himself by pouring a bottle of milkshake into two wine glasses. He cleans the rims with his sleeve. He finishes the bottle himself. He then opens a packet of bourbons and begins piling them on to a plate, trying to build them into a pyramid. He fails several times. He goes to the door and opens it.* ALICE *storms past him into the centre of the room.*)

Are you OK?
ALICE: Yes!
CHARLIE: Alroight… do you want to sit down?
ALICE: Yes. (*She does. She rises immediately.*) No, I do not. Wait, do I? (*She sits back down.*) OK, yeah.

(CHARLIE *stands awkwardly.*)

Things haven't changed much here.
CHARLIE: The wallpaper was my idea.
ALICE: Very... sophisticated. (*She looks down at the wine glasses.*) You made cocktails?
CHARLIE: No. It's milkshake – like we used to drink!
ALICE: Oh yeah. Cool pyramid. (*She takes one from the top.*) Thank god I didn't take one from the bottom! (*She laughs.*) Would have ended up with a nightmarish game of bourbon Jenga.
CHARLIE: Well, I do have Twister.

(ALICE *stops laughing awkwardly.*)

That was a joke.
ALICE: Oh. (*She swallows the rest of the biscuit and picks up the wine glass.*) Shall we toast to something, then?
CHARLIE: How about...
ALICE: To old friends? (*They chink and have a slug.*) I'm sorry.
CHARLIE: It's OK. (*Slight pause.*) You should know, all of what she said back there...
ALICE: Please – I know it wasn't true.
CHARLIE: I would never—
ALICE: Let's talk about something else. Didn't you have a house party here once?
CHARLIE: Yeah. Once. That's why I redecorated. It was a big job. I'm still paying for it!
ALICE: Wow.
CHARLIE: My mum found the cigarette butts in her Haku-Jo.

SCENE TEN: FRIENDS

ALICE: Her what?
CHARLIE: Um, it's a fancy cactus. (*He points to a corner.*) It used to be over there.

(ALICE *looks in the direction he's pointing. She remembers.*)

ALICE: Oh, Jesus. Wasn't that… yeah, it was!
CHARLIE: Oh, no…
ALICE: It was the night Jordan thought he was Batman – I blame the blueberry vodka – and we were trying to explain to him he wasn't, and he kept saying 'I cannot be stopped! I cannot be stopped! I am Batman. My parents will be avenged!'… 'No Jordan! You are not a superhero!' we kept screaming. 'Batman is not a superhero – he is a crime fighter!' He had enough brains to contemplate the complexity of his alter ego, but not enough to stop fantasising. And he genuinely thought he was invincible. Immortal. We all were. And we were soaked up with anything we could get our hands on. And Jordan kept shouting 'I CAN'T BE STOPPED! I CAN'T BE STOPPED! NOTHING CAN BEAT ME!' So someone says, 'Oh yeah? I bet that window can stop you, Batman,' and of course Bat-Jordan is taking none of this and screams 'SOME WINDOW AIN'T GONNA STOP ME!' and jumps on to the table littered with cups, butts and cards, runs along it and propels himself off the corner and through that goddam window. Glass has gone everywhere, and it all feels like it should be in slow motion, you know? And they're all cheering him on – 'JORDAN! JORDAN! JORDAN!' Shards of glass

were all over the carpet and table and we danced over them like glitter, like broken stars fallen from the sky. And Jordan's face is all cut up, and we are chanting at him outside, but he doesn't get up. He's not Batman. He's not flying away. He's fallen through Charlie's mum's front window and into her rockery.

CHARLIE: That was Liam, not Jordan.
ALICE: Are you sure?
CHARLIE: Yeah.

(*Slight pause.*)

ALICE: Your parents have done it up since I was here last.
CHARLIE: That was me.
ALICE: You did all of this?
CHARLIE: Yeah.
ALICE: Wow – it's really good.
CHARLIE: Don't sound too surprised.
ALICE: Sorry, it's just… it's *really* good. You should do this properly – like, as a job or something.
CHARLIE: The careers woman told me 'Farmer' was more… 'achievable' with my grades.
ALICE: Maybe she was wrong. You could have been—
CHARLIE: I dunno.
ALICE: I didn't mean 'better'.

(*Slight pause.*)

CHARLIE: I didn't think you did.
ALICE: Shit. Now I feel like a wanker telling you what to do – as if I know what I'm doing. I don't know

SCENE TEN: FRIENDS

anything. Things are simpler up here. I'm trying to get used to it again.

CHARLIE: Well, you sound like one now. But oi don't think it's simpler or easier 'ere. People wherever you go are so little inside. Oi missed you too, by the way, if you were gonna say tha'.

(Pause. The following should be delivered in a different voice – the voices of their past selves. As it goes on, ALICE *becomes more and more Norfolk-accented.)*

Oi miss singin' rubbish pop songs wi' you from Radio 1Extra.

ALICE: I miss putting lip gloss on in the Spar before school.

CHARLIE: When we agreed our biggest win in year ten was findin' the best chips in Norfolk.

ALICE: Asking you to cut my hair once and you gave me a micro fringe.

CHARLIE: I miss stealing those little pots of milk you get and suckin' them on the swings.

ALICE: Oi miss your freckles.

CHARLIE: Oi miss you holdin' my hand when I 'ad moi braces taken off, holding moi hand when I 'ad moi ears pierced and—

ALICE: And you holdin' moine when Rob Willis dumped me the noight before the French oral.

CHARLIE: Ha. French oral.

ALICE: Shut up!

CHARLIE: Oi miss sharin' the same roll-on deodorant on the school bus.

FRIDGE

ALICE: Becoz we both forgot to in the mornin's.
CHARLIE: We stank!
ALICE: You did more!
CHARLIE: No, you did!

(*They smile and begin laughing.*)

BOTH: It was called... Manhattan Sunrise!

(*Pause.*)

ALICE: Or when oi got the letter sayin' oi got into Wyndham! You were so 'appy for me!
LO: That was the beginning. Mum went travelling more.
CHARLIE: Yeah, until oi realoised moi best friend woz never goin' t' be the same agen.
ALICE: Oi came back in the holidays.
CHARLIE: You were different. You 'ad new friends.
ALICE: You wouldn't've got on wi' 'em.
CHARLIE: You stopped talkin' t' me after a whoile.
ALICE: An' you were busy wi' yer apprenticeship.
CHARLIE: Sure. Wouldn't wanna get in the way o' moi career, would yer?

(*They look at each other. The fridge shakes.*)

I should feed the sow.
ALICE: Oh, sure. (*He goes to get the utensils, a bottle, powder and spoon.*) Can I help?
CHARLIE: Alroight.

SCENE TEN: FRIENDS

(*As he goes back and forth, she sets to, clearing the bourbons and glasses. They work around each other.*)

    Need to add the powder. Vitamins, y'see. (*He lays it all in front of them. He gives her the spoon.*) 'Ere. You measure. Seven of 'em. I'll measure the milk. (*She does so. He does the same.*) And make it level!
ALICE: Sorry. I don't think I'm any good at this.
CHARLIE: You're doing foine.
ALICE: Funny.

(*She begins to level them as* CHARLIE *holds the bottle. They put both in together.*)

CHARLIE: Gently!

(*They continue doing this for the following.*)

ALICE: Where are your 'rents?
CHARLIE: Moved out. Dad still helps, but Mum can't handle the cold no more. Fires aren't enough for the bones.
ALICE: So, just you?

(*He nods. They continue.*)

CHARLIE: You sound roight posh now.
ALICE: It's just…
CHARLIE: I heard yer. Very important-sounding.
ALICE: It's for the job.
CHARLIE: And that would be…?

FRIDGE

ALICE: Don't laugh.
CHARLIE: I knew it! You're a stripper!
ALICE: Oh, shut up!
CHARLIE: Oi! Careful!
ALICE: I sell staycation holidays to here.

(CHARLIE *laughs.*)

    I know. It's sad.
CHARLIE: No, it's not. Means you still like this place a little bit. (*They finish measuring.*) And done! Thanks.

(ALICE*'s phone rings. The fridge shakes. She misses the call.*)

ALICE: I need to go. Maybe another time.

(ALICE *walks to the door, picks up her coat and is rummaging for her keys.* CHARLIE *stops.*)

CHARLIE: I think I like you again.

(*Pause.*)

ALICE: I don't know whether to process the 'like' or the 'again' of that sentence.
CHARLIE: Oh, come on, Alice, I gave you my footie socks to wear on your hands so they wouldn't get cold, I let you borrow my bike helmet home, I let you have the bigger half of my fish-finger sandwich… (*Pause.*) Well, now I feel like a complete prat.
ALICE: You're not a prat. I… I'm flattered, Charlie, but…

SCENE TEN: FRIENDS

CHARLIE: 'I'm flattered, Charlie'. Christ, just forget it.
ALICE: Charlie!
CHARLIE: As if I could make you happy. As if.

(*Silence.* ALICE *moves to him slowly. They kiss slowly, intimately.*
LO *runs in as they kiss. She stares at them.*)

LO: The door was open.

(*They break away from each other.*)

You were taking your time. I'll… I'll just go.

(*She runs out.*)

ALICE: Thanks a lot!
CHARLIE: ME?
ALICE: Yeah, you with all your fish-finger courting!
CHARLIE: You kissed me!
ALICE: Yeah, well, what do you think she's going to do now after seeing that?
CHARLIE: You started it!
ALICE: Because of you! And now she's—
CHARLIE: I know, Alice.
ALICE: Use your imagination.
CHARLIE: Yes, I know, Alice. I know! Oh shit.

(ALICE *hides her head in her hands.*)

I can't do this any more.
ALICE: I left because I couldn't take playing Mother any more. It's so flat here, Charlie. I can't stand it. The

people are flat. I wanted more. I'm sorry if that's not good enough for you. Lo still thinks I'm going to save her from herself all over again... when the truth is I can barely save myself.

CHARLIE: We're all she has that keeps her here.

ALICE: I've done this before without help. I don't... I can't do 'we'.

CHARLIE: Well, I'm happy with you and Lo if you want it to be.

(Silence. LO enters, unseen to them. She watches them, as before. The blue of the fridge intensifies, and she watches them as though watching a TV.)

I have this dream. This dream where I'm dyeing my cheeks red. Bled for the other half of me. You're there now, in the dream. It used to be just me. Not any more. We spindle the empty wind but there is only green there; we weave the wind into words, splice them up for our teeth. Mince the tongues around us wagging. And stuff our mouths a-plenty. And then there's weeds – weeds growing in our pockets. I keep pulling at them, but they just grow back like trees in our pockets. I catch them.

ALICE: I play with them.

CHARLIE: With you. Play them in the grey air the shit's spat out on. Play the shit for pocket green.

BOTH: And you're smiling. You're smiling at me.

CHARLIE: And you're still smiling, still smiling, my Alice.

ALICE: Who always dreams good things?

SCENE TEN: FRIENDS

(*Pause. The TV-like light goes out.* LO *leaves.*)

CHARLIE: I'm going to go now. That sow needs feedin'.
(*He takes the bottle of formula.*)
ALICE: No wait, Charlie—
CHARLIE: Well, go after her! Go *home*, Alice.
ALICE: She's attention-seeking. It'll only make things worse.
CHARLIE: You can't be serious?
ALICE: It's just like when we were little and I'd tell her the story of—
CHARLIE: I can't believe you're her sister!

(*He storms past her and exits after* LO. ALICE *kicks the fridge hard, angrily.*)

ALICE: Fuck!

SCENE ELEVEN

Stars

Outside. The night sky above. LO *is sitting on a pot on the patio, looking up at the stars.* CHARLIE *appears and sees her. He stands by, calmly.*

LO (*quietly crying*): Sometimes I come out here just to look up and see nothing. Have you noticed how many stars there are in a Norfolk sky?

CHARLIE: I—

LO: I am having a moment.

CHARLIE: Oh. Sorry. So, do you want me to go? (*Pause.*) Have you had your moment now? (*He turns to leave, but she catches him.*)

LO: You're not good at being sad, are you?

CHARLIE: What's the right answer to that?

LO: Was that your best shot?

CHARLIE: You're not getting better, are you?

(*Slight pause.*)

LO: So. You like my sister? You going to get married? Have kids? Move in? The whole dream? We could play the end credits for you both.

CHARLIE: No, thanks... and thanks for your accusation earlier.
LO: Sorry about that.
CHARLIE (*shrugs*): Oh, look – Orion!

(*He joins her and they look up at it.*)

    I just kissed her is all.
LO: Charlie.
CHARLIE: OK, I like her a lot. A lot.
LO: Knew it!
CHARLIE: She didn't come back for me, you know.
LO: She belongs here. Like you and me.
CHARLIE: She's really messed up with this...
LO: This...?
CHARLIE: Well, what you are.
LO: What I 'am'?
CHARLIE: I don't know the politically correct thing I'm supposed to call you.

(LO *stares him down, then up at the night sky.* CHARLIE *plays with the formula bottle.*)

LO: She was always going to be our star. The first time she ever caught me. I was in the bath – bubbles, candles, whale music, the fully-loaded, you know. I poured this shea and coconut bath thing into the water – I'd got it for my birthday but didn't really know how to use it. Biggest bubbles ever, mind you. So big I could see my reflection in them – so many reflections staring back at me like pink funhouse

SCENE ELEVEN: STARS

mirrors – and the smell of coconuts hung in the air. (*Pause.*) Have you ever had the urge to just keep your head underwater and stay there? See what happens. Have you ever held your head against the bottom of the bath, opened your eyes and looked up through the water and scream? No one can hear you. No one. And you've locked the door, so no one can touch you down there. Warm and safe. But it's when you run out of scream and coconut-soap water rushes into your lungs and ears and nose, and you've got to decide whether to come up, follow instinct, or embrace the temptation to simply stay down there, untouched, unheard. So now I'm lying in what I feel is a soapy amniotic sac in my bath, and I can feel the funhouse bubbles foaming like oxygen into my foetal little body. And I see the razor in the corner, and I take it into the water. I take it and it feels so good. It feels so good. I watch the coconut bath swirl with blood, and it looks like raspberry ripple. It's dark and warm and sickly sweet, but I don't want to stop pretending. And my whale music has switched to a Disney album and I shudder, cos it's so sweet – it's sickly like the water now. I'm laughing. I'm laughing cos it's too perfect. It's too ironic, too perfect. That sticky, sweet American singing voice. It's diabetes for my ears. And it's fine things are blurring, it's fine that the water has thickened now, deep red, and I've managed to blunt the razor; it's fine because she's singing and there's nothing wrong. And I thought of Alice. And a calm takes over me. I'm not drowning, I'm just breathing bubbles, I'm just floating upside down, dreaming. I'm the Little Mermaid. Sounds pathetic, doesn't it? I'd laugh at me. It is pathetic. Trying to kill yourself with Disney in the background. I never did grow up. The privileged millennials, drifting around, floating upside down, not knowing what to do with ourselves – except put Disney on repeat until we feel like a princess again.

(*Silence.*)

They all just leave. (*She starts to cry.*) We all just drift away. I wish I had. A long, long time ago.
CHARLIE: I know.
LO: No, you don't.
CHARLIE: Yeah, I do.
LO: And what makes you the expert on me?
CHARLIE: A lot, actually.
LO: But you're Charlie. Charlie, who ploughs and sows and checks in on everyone – even that old biddy raptor lady. Charlie who can open a tinnie with his Canaries key chain one handed. You don't get—
CHARLIE: Oh, oi can't, can oi? I'm not allowed to, am oi? What would 'appen if oi weren't 'ere? Too few care after so many have gone.

(LO *stares up at the stars again.*)

I was up near the fork 'fore Marriott's Way one day, and oi was the only one out there. Mindin' it all, oi were. Nothing was taller than me for moiles.

SCENE ELEVEN: STARS

The skies lied flat in front of me. And oi thought, I'll never feel as important as oi do now. And oi didn't know if I was going to feel like it again. And for a second, not even that – I mean, I had thought of this before, who doesn't, but oi... And then the land's work ate me up all over again and I forgot all about it. Until the next time I was in the fields alone. Oi don't think I've ever said that out loud before. Ever.

LO: Thanks. I know everyone is worrying about me, but I worry about you.
CHARLIE: Thanks for being here for me too.
LO: Alice used to be.
CHARLIE: But she's come back to us.
LO: To you.
CHARLIE: You don't believe that, do you?

(LO *suddenly grabs hold of* CHARLIE *in a hug. He tentatively pats her head.*)

I don't think so.
LO: She's never scared.
CHARLIE: Oi think she feared losing you.
LO: No she doesn't.
CHARLIE: Even us out here get scared. It's what's hayre when we go home that's scarier.

(*Pause.*)

You want to play a game?
LO (*sniffs*): OK. Which one?

CHARLIE: I dunno. What do you want to play?

(LO *stares at* CHARLIE. *She suddenly breaks away from his embrace. The following should be over-dramatised, like children playing out scenes from a film.*)

LO: I regard myself an upright and rational mer-king, but I set rules for a reason, and I expect you to stick to them.
CHARLIE: What are you doing?
LO: Playing.
CHARLIE: What are we playing?
LO: I'm the Mer-King. You're the Little Mermaid, my daughter.
CHARLIE: But why am I—
LO: Don't say 'the girl', because you're not! You're a mermaid.

(CHARLIE *stares at her.*)

Like, you're a mermaid, not a farmer… (*Slight pause.*) Am I to believe that you saved a human prince from being drowned? (*Slight pause.*) Say 'But I had to! I couldn't let him drown!'
CHARLIE: But I had to! I couldn't let him drown…!
LO: But you know that you aren't permitted to communicate with the upperworld! One day in 365, that's the rule – and no contact!
CHARLIE: Oh, I know this! (LO *shoots him a look, and he changes his voice to sound like a little mermaid might for her approval.*) But if I didn't save him he would have died!

SCENE ELEVEN: STARS

LO: And what concern of ours is it if he did?

CHARLIE: How can you say that?

LO: Because I know human beings... and what they're capable of!

CHARLIE: But I love her!

LO: No...! No...! For god's sake, Charlie, have you lost your senses completely? *He's* the human – *you're* the mermaid!

CHARLIE: Oh yes... Well, I had to save him!

LO: Enough! I won't hear another word on the subject...! OK, now you – the Little Mermaid – leave him, um, me, and then he, I, doesn't go after you cos I'm so angry with you. And you... she'll never see him – or anyone else again – and she doesn't even care!

(LO *begins to 'blast' things with her 'trident' – she tarts pointing at things and making them 'explode'; she takes the pill sheets and throws them on the floor, 'destroying them'.*)

CHARLIE: No... No! Lo, stop...! Lo, stop...!

(CHARLIE *picks up the sheets of pills in desperation. He restrains* LO *as she struggles to free herself, panting and squirming.* CHARLIE *eventually releases her and* LO *runs to the fridge, forces the door open and climbs in.* LO *is panting, exhausted, within. Pause.*)

Hey. Hey!

LO (*from inside*): GO AWAY!

(CHARLIE *goes towards the fridge, kneeling.*)

CHARLIE: I didn't mean to.

(*Silence.*)

You won't tell anyone my secret, will you? I'm trusting you, Lo.

(*She opens the door. He leads her slowly out of the fridge, and she falls into his chest. Her breathing normalises in small gasps.*)

LO: I promise.

(ALICE *enters.*)

ALICE: Lo!

(LO *and* CHARLIE *break away from one another.* LO *runs out past* ALICE.)

CHARLIE: You need to talk to her.
ALICE: That's all I need. You are encouraging her!
CHARLIE: I'm done helping!
ALICE: She doesn't need your help.
CHARLIE: How do you know what she needs? You haven't been around!
ALICE: I don't need you coming in here and hyping her up like that.
CHARLIE: Go after her, then, all over again. (*Slight pause.*) GO!

SCENE ELEVEN: STARS

(ALICE *exits after* LO. CHARLIE *is left alone. He looks out to where she has left the stage, and then sits on top of the fridge. Perhaps he stands to look at the sky. Pause. Then he jumps off.*)

    I loved you once.
    I loved you
    When I couldn't see to live.
    When living was loving
    And loving you lit us up;
    Our love taught us
    To love ourselves,
    And we did,
    We
    So
    So
    Loved
    And
    Laid
    And
    Learnt to live.
    If I am silent now
    Do not think I am mute.
    If I am still
    Do not think I am empty.
    If I smile now
    Do not think I have
    No tears left.
    Because I have all and more.
    Much
    More.
    Much

FRIDGE

More
To
Love
You
All
Over
Again.

(He picks the formula bottle up and leaves.)

SCENE TWELVE

Out

The lights come up on ALICE *and* LO*'s kitchen. They storm in at the same time.* LO *starts pacing up and down.*

LO: So, you want to talk? OK. Let's talk. Let's talk.

ALICE: Sudden change of heart?

LO: We only had me to talk about then. But now, we have my sister hanging off Charlie's face to contend with.

ALICE: I didn't mean for you to see.

LO: I get it!

ALICE: If you've got something to say—

LO: Yeah I do. Why are you here? No no no no... why are you here NOW? All you've done is come back and fuck up mine – and Charlie's – life all over again.

ALICE: I didn't mean to break his heart!

LO: I'm talking about me! Stop making it about you all the time!

ALICE: That's...

(*Pause.* LO *sighs, running her hands through her hair.*)

I came back for you.

LO: All right, but he's the reason you're staying. (LO *starts hyperventilating.*)

ALICE: Breathe! Drink. Live. Jesus.

LO: I can't, Alice, I can't breathe! Alice, I can't breathe!

ALICE: For fuck's sake. Drink this.

(*She hands* LO *a bottle of clear liquid.*)

LO (*spitting it out*): What was that?

ALICE: Water. What's wrong – not your usual sweet stuff?

LO: Oh, come on – you know me better than that, Big Sis!

(ALICE *takes a bottle of vodka from the fridge.* LO *grabs the bottle before* ALICE *can begin to pour it into glasses and swigs from it.* ALICE *takes it from her and does the same.*)

Impressive. We're definitely from the same DNA puddle, you and me.

ALICE: Gene pool. It's gene pool!

LO: Oh yeah, shit. I never use the right words at the right time. You seem to be an expert, though.

ALICE: This isn't about *my* fuck-ups, Lo, this is about yours.

LO: Because I'm always the problem child.

(ALICE *swigs again. They look at each other intensely, and then burst out laughing at the honesty of their exchange. They lean against the fridge. They relax for the first time.*)

SCENE TWELVE: OUT

ALICE: I'm surprised, this time, I've got to say – I thought you would've gone for wine for the tenth attempt. Was it a special one this time to finally get me back here?

LO: It was special, yes. But not to get you back. That's a lost cause now. I had Charlie to thank for that, remember? And nope – thought I'd break tradition. I'm playing with the big boys now.

ALICE: Give it to me.

LO: Bottom cupboard's a mini fucking wine cellar for Mum to come home to and wallow in over the state of her life.

ALICE: Huh.

LO: Yeah, Sauvignon Blanc goes well with a couple of sheets of aspirin, too.

ALICE: Stop it.

LO: Too much for you? *(She feigns a smile.)*

ALICE: Sometimes I wonder if you were adopted. Really.

LO: Wow. I'm the princess here, not you!

ALICE: Yeah, in your tower, with nothing to do but eat and drink yourself stupid alone like a little pig.

LO: I can do more!

ALICE: Yeah, go slaughter yourself.

LO: That's great. Thanks, Mummy. I'll work on that. I must make you so proud.

ALICE: I'm your sister!

LO: That's getting really tired now.

(ALICE *is silent.*)

Oh my fucking god. You're not crying, are you? What about old Charlie boy, eh? He's part of the family now! Let's get him in here to dry them.

ALICE: I finished it with him. I said things.

LO: Really?

ALICE: I don't know. Maybe. Maybe not.

LO: You did?

ALICE: Yes.

LO: Had enough of playing happy families?

ALICE: That's not fair.

LO: You. Me. Him. It almost felt 'normal' again, you know? It almost felt like family.

(*Pause.*)

Don't judge me. And don't tell me about what's not fair! I didn't ask you to come here to judge me, Alice.

ALICE: You didn't do much asking, did you? You know what some of my friends said? They said, 'Don't go. Cos if you do, it'll just tell her that every time she does it, you'll come running.'

LO: Look at you. Doing some hard thinking.

ALICE: I'm just trying to understand it all over again.

LO: You don't like this, do you? Coming back to this place that you called home – you hate it.

ALICE: I think you've had enough. (ALICE *takes the bottle from her.*)

LO: You hate it, don't you? Being there for someone. Someone depending on you, looking to you. Cos being you must be so damn hard. (*She laughs darkly.*) You know… you are just like Chrissy.

SCENE TWELVE: OUT

(ALICE *slams the bottle down on the top of the fridge.*)

    Drank to the bottom of the bottle—
ALICE: Mum. She was still—
LO: Just so she couldn't see Dad's face any more. Where were you?
ALICE: I was a mess then, Lo; I had to get out of here—
LO: And you couldn't afford to take your baby sister with you?
ALICE: I was unpredictable then!
LO: Well, guess what? Maybe I feel a little unpredictable now.

(LO *goes to the fridge, takes the bottle of vodka from the top and pours it over herself, then takes a lighter from her pocket. She presses her thumb on the lighter. Silence.*)

    I will.
ALICE: I believe you.
LO: I will. I'm not fucking around.
ALICE: I know.
LO: You've got to kill the runt to save the drift. Just like Charlie said.
ALICE: Is this what you want?
LO: You made me. You might as well light me up, Big Sis.

(ALICE *walks over to* LO *and takes the vodka bottle from her, then pours the rest over herself.*)

ALICE: I made you, huh? (*She slaps her and then hugs her intensely.*) I love you. I fucking love you, and if you want to go, I'm going with you this time. You can take me cos I never took you when I left. We're the family. Us two. Forget Mum, forget Dad, forget Charlie. We're going together this time!

(LO *cries uncontrollably into* ALICE*'s arms.* ALICE *kisses* LO*'s head.* ALICE *takes the lighter from* LO, *her thumb on it. Pause.* ALICE *throws it away and breaks away from* LO, *moving towards the door.* LO *goes to the fridge. She opens the door to go in, but freezes on the precipice of doing so.*)

Come with me.
LO: What?
ALICE: Please?
LO: I…
ALICE: It's just a fridge, Lo.

(LO *runs over to* ALICE. *They exit. Darkness. From the darkness,* CHARLIE *comes on. The wind blows, as before; he fights it. He has found the sow dead.*)

CHARLIE: Oh, girl, no. Not you.

(*He looks around the kitchen, at the mess, at the fridge. He runs to the fridge and knocks. No answer. He looks inside. Nothing.*)

If I'd just got there sooner… Alice… Lo! (*A thought occurs to him. He runs out.*) Alice! Alice! Lo!

(*Darkness; wind howls.*)

SCENE THIRTEEN

Stop

ALICE *and* LO *are sitting at the bus shelter, waiting for a bus to arrive. They are both still wet from the vodka.* LO *sits on top of the fridge, swaying her legs.*

ALICE (*waving her phone in the air*): Where is that signal? I swear it was in this spot before!
LO (*pointing*): Try over there.

(*She moves off a little.*)

ALICE: Nothing. So much for a dramatic exit from this place.
LO: It was never going to be one of your stories.
ALICE: Urgh. I just wish it would be for once, though.

(LO *sulks in the shelter.* ALICE *lights a cigarette. Pause.*)

LO: What are we doing?
ALICE: I'm making it up as I go along. (ALICE *gets her phone out and throws it to* LO.)

LO: Watch it!
ALICE: Leave Mum a voicemail.
LO: But what if—
ALICE: Do it.
LO: Fine. It's dialling... what do I say...? I'm with the Mermaid of Shipden! (*She hangs up.*) What?
ALICE (*smoking*): I'm going to be blamed for this, I just know it... Great... um... (*She gives* LO *a look.*) She'll think you've drowned or something!
LO: So? She deserves it.
ALICE: Nu-uh.

(ALICE *points at the phone.* LO *throws it back.* ALICE *dials quickly. She smokes her cigarette.*)

(*Callously:*) Lo's with me.

(*She hangs up and puts the phone back in her pocket. She takes a last drag on her cigarette and stubs it out. Beyond the bus shelter and bushes,* LO *hears rustling and looks over.* ALICE *doesn't.* CHARLIE *enters, scratched and tousled from the undergrowth. He is out of breath. He is unseen by* ALICE.)

LO: Alice! Why'd you do that?
ALICE: You know why.

(*She goes to take another cigarette from the box with her mouth.*)

CHARLIE: Those'll kill yer.
ALICE: Why does he have to be so—
CHARLIE: Alice?

SCENE THIRTEEN: STOP

ALICE: What do you want?

(LO *snatches* ALICE's *cigarette box out of her hand and plays with her lighter, then moves back to the shelter.*)

   (*Whispers:*) We settled this. I know what I'm doing. Me and Lo are leaving, and you're not coming. Remember?

CHARLIE: The sow, she's—

ALICE: Yep?

CHARLIE (*breathless*): The sow. She's... she's dead. Oi found her last noight. She's dead.

ALICE (*turning*): How? What?

LO (*rising*): Oh Charlie!

CHARLIE: Not yous to worry. Moi fault. Oi shoulda been more attentive to her.

ALICE: Now what? Do you want us to—

CHARLIE: No, oi dunno... oi just needed to tell someone. So someone besides me knew.

LO: Charlie?

CHARLIE: We move on. But, y'know...

ALICE: It was a pig, Charlie...

CHARLIE: She's got me thinkin' 'bout things.

LO: Is there a bus soon? I'm just gonna check the times... (*She goes back to the shelter and returns to her spot on top of the fridge.*)

CHARLIE: What am I to you? You, here now, and Lo... I want to do this with you – and Lo, if she will let me.

ALICE: Am I the pig in all of this?

CHARLIE: No!

FRIDGE

ALICE: Well, I don't need a shoulder to cry on.
CHARLIE: Yeah.

(*Pause. He looks over to* LO, *swaying her legs, pretending not to hear.*)

>You don't need to be strong all the time, you know. You...

ALICE: Yes?
CHARLIE: You are...
ALICE: Yes...
CHARLIE: I love you.
ALICE: OH FUCK.
CHARLIE: What?
ALICE: What?
CHARLIE: I love you.
ALICE: You do?
CHARLIE: Yep.
ALICE: Wow.
CHARLIE: And?
ALICE: And?

(LO *finds a milkshake and slurps it, watching them.*)

CHARLIE: Well...
ALICE: Don't bully me into loving you!
CHARLIE: I'm not.
ALICE: Good. Because I do.
CHARLIE: What?
ALICE (*shifting uncomfortably, struggling for each word*): I do... the same... with you... that way.

SCENE THIRTEEN: STOP

(*Pause.*)

CHARLIE: Wait, what was that?
ALICE: I... feel the same way, then.
CHARLIE: Whoi can't you just say it?
ALICE: I just did.
CHARLIE: No, you didn't.
ALICE: Yeah, I did.
CHARLIE: Not properly.
ALICE: Fine. (*Sighs.*) I love you.

(LO *sniggers.*)

CHARLIE: That was convincing.
ALICE: I said it!
CHARLIE: That was not an 'I love you'.
ALICE: How then?
CHARLIE: Like you *do*.
ALICE (*inhales*): I don't know what that is.
CHARLIE: Yes you do.

(*He walks towards her, takes her head in his hands and draws her closer. His hands run through her hair.*)

I love you.

(*He suddenly steps away, turning his back on her and losing all intimacy. He stands back triumphantly.*)

See? That wasn't too difficult, was it?

FRIDGE

ALICE: You arrogant little prince. I have loved harder than you ever have, and I have lost more than you ever had. I hurt. It rips me apart every day knowing that I can't make *her* happy. Everything she does I feel – the sudden drop and I can't stop. And then you come along, thinking you belong, playing happy families with a broken one. So am I the fantasist now? Pretending we're something we're not? Make-believing, repeating, cos this boy, this man, has made me feel normal for the first time. I've dropped my guard. No longer falling apart. I saved her and you've saved me. We need each other. All of us. All three of us. We're building it back, the three of us. And I love him for that. I fucking love him for that. I love him. I love him. I love you.

(CHARLIE *looks at her. He smiles.* ALICE *smiles back.*)

CHARLIE: But I can't leave here. This land *is* me. I'm… asking you to…
ALICE: Next time I'm back, maybe we could…
CHARLIE: That would be nice.
ALICE: Nice?
CHARLIE: Here we bloody go.
ALICE: We can share her.
CHARLIE: We can do this.

(*The sound of a bus. Pause.*)

LO: Quick! You two, a bus is coming! A bus is finally coming! Flag it down! Stop! Stop!

SCENE THIRTEEN: STOP

ALICE: It's not that far, really! When you think about it…
LO: No, but you'll be back!
CHARLIE: Yes, she bloody will!
LO: We're family now.
ALICE: Come with me.
LO: Who, me?
CHARLIE: You two should go.
LO: All of us?
ALICE (*looking at* CHARLIE): Why not?
CHARLIE: Stop!

(*They all look at each other. They all try to flag the bus down with waving arms and calls.*)

ALL: Stop! Stop! STOP!

(LO, ALICE *and* CHARLIE *all continue to call after the bus.*)

LO: What happens now, Alice?
ALICE: Well, what do you want? It's our story!
LO: Oi rewind it to the beginning!
ALICE (*laughing*): And start all over again!

(LO *and* ALICE *hug. Then* ALICE *and* CHARLIE *do. They all continue flagging the bus down as if they are waving. Perhaps music plays in rapture à la end credits. The fridge blares blue. A knock ricochets through the space.* LO *freezes.*)

LO: Did you hear that?
CHARLIE: It's here! Get on! Get on!
ALICE: I'll cover everyone!

FRIDGE

LO: Can't you hear?

(*They stare at her. The wind howls in the distance and something like a moan is heard.*)

    Nothing. You came back.
ALICE: You got out.
LO: It's nothing.
ALICE AND CHARLIE: Well, come on!

(*Fade to darkness.*)

ACKNOWLEDGEMENTS

Tonje Wik Olaussen read many many versions of this script and gave me a chance in North London. Thank you. Thank you to Leo Garrick and Pippa Davis for being keen critics and great company on show nights; to Mary O'Loan for laughing and crying with me, and for being my dear friend. Actors Siân Bennett, Therica Wilson-Read, Arthur Velarde, Rachel Hosker were so giving in R&Ds in pubs. I am grateful to Phoebe Robinson for the music and storytelling.

Without the kindness and intelligence of Will Dady, my editor and publisher, I could not have completed this. My sister and mother are my foundation, on which most of my writing rests. And as Stephen Fry says, 'Norfolk's not all soft and lovely. It doesn't ask to be loved.'

OTHER TITLES FROM RENARD PRESS

ISBN: 9781913724092
224pp • Paperback • £7.99

ISBN: 9781913724023
80pp • Paperback • £6.99

ISBN: 9781913724085
224pp • Paperback • £6.99

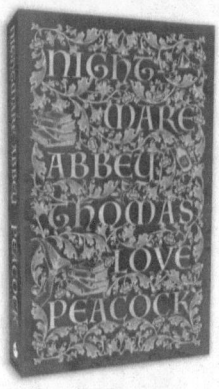

ISBN: 9781913724078
160pp • Paperback • £7.99

ISBN: 9781913724061
160pp • Paperback • £7.99

ISBN: 9781913724115
128pp • Paperback • £7.99

DISCOVER THE FULL COLLECTION AT
WWW.RENARDPRESS.COM

www.ingramcontent.com/pod-product-compliance
Lightning Source LLC
Chambersburg PA
CBHW011318080526
44589CB00020B/2749